home sweet home
cross stitch

home sweet home
 cross stitch

D&C
David and Charles
www.rucraft.com

To dear little Charlie, with all my love

A DAVID & CHARLES BOOK
Copyright © David & Charles Limited 2010

David & Charles is an F+W Media Inc. company
4700 East Galbraith Road, Cincinnati, OH 45236

First published in the UK and US in 2010

Text and designs copyright © Helen Philipps 2010
Layout and photography copyright © David & Charles 2010

Helen Philipps has asserted her right to be identified as author
of this work in accordance with the Copyright, Designs and Patents Act, 1988.

A catalogue record for this book is available from the British Library.

ISBN-13: 978-0-7153-3290-0 paperback
ISBN-10: 0-7153-3290-2 paperback

Printed in China by RR Donnelley
for David & Charles
Brunel House   Newton Abbot   Devon

Acquisitions Editors Cheryl Brown and Jennifer Fox-Proverbs
Editorial Assistant Jeni Hennah
Project Editor and Chart Preparation Lin Clements
Designer Mia Farrant
Photographer Simon Whitmore
Production Controller Kelly Smith
Pre-Press Natasha Jorden

www.davidandcharles.co.uk

David & Charles publish high quality books on a wide range of subjects.
For more great book ideas visit:
www.rubooks.co.uk

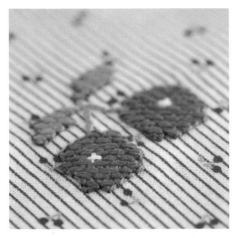

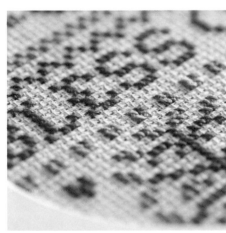

CONTENTS

Welcome Home

Our homes have always been important to us, and we enjoy making them comfortable and stylish for ourselves and our families. This book celebrates all the delights of the home in cross stitch projects, with a collection of charming designs celebrating a variety of different homes.

We start with a sweet sampler in sugared almond colours using the most famous sampler saying, Home Sweet Home, which can be personalized with your name and dates. Home Is Where You Hang Your Heart is a fresh little contemporary sampler with a three-dimensional stitched heart to hang from a button. In the Comforts of Home chapter two funky cushions are embellished with appliqué flowers, hearts and yo-yos. The gorgeous French-style red and white sampler features a house reminiscent of a French chateau. For a country look, two companion samplers, Welcome to Our House and Bless Our House, use rustic-looking fabrics and soft, countryside colours. The Heart of the Home sampler has been made up as a delightful little hanger that's perfect for your kitchen. Home is Where the Heart Is has a fresh, modern feel with rows of pastel-coloured houses. Finally, All Hearts Come Home at Christmas, with its warm colours and cosy festive feel, rounds off a collection of fun and contemporary cross stitch designs that are a delight to stitch.

There is also an attractive range of smaller projects, which are quick and easy to stitch and would make lovely gifts and keepsakes. Advice on materials, techniques and making up is given at the end.

Surely the perfect way for stitchers to turn any house into a home!

Home Sweet Home

Home Sweet Home

This sampler takes its inspiration from the classic home-loving sampler saying but gives it a fresh, new feel. The little pink house with its picket fence and flowering tree epitomizes the cosy little home of our dreams. The pretty flowers and the shelf of homely knick-knacks accentuate the charms of nest building. This design uses variegated thread in the foliage and lemon seed beads in the flower centres to add extra interest, while the candy-coloured star buttons provide an extra sweet touch. Make the sampler your very own by changing the name and date using the alphabet and numbers provided.

A Home Sweet Home hanger on page 14 uses just the sentiment from the main chart and is a really quick project to make. The sentiment is stitched and mounted on a pretty hanger, which is then embellished with beads, card flowers and ribbon.

This charming sampler is very easy to stitch — just whole cross stitch and some backstitch outlining. The little seed beads bring an extra sparkle but you could work French knots instead if you prefer. Change the name and date by using the alphabet and numbers provided.

Make this cosy sampler your very own by customizing the name and date using the alphabet and numbers charted on page 19. The graph paper provided will allow you to plan your wording.

Home Sweet Home Sampler

Stitch count
112 high x 66 wide

Finished size
20.3 x 12cm (8 x 4¾in)

You will need
- 28-count white linen 30.5 x 23cm (12 x 9in)
- DMC stranded cotton (floss) and Color Variations thread as listed in chart key
- Tapestry needle size 24–26 and a beading needle
- Mill Hill seed beads 02002 lemon
- Three candy-pink star buttons (HobbyCraft – see Suppliers)

1 Prepare your fabric for work and begin stitching in the centre of the fabric and from the centre of the chart on page 16/17.

2 Stitch over two threads of linen using two strands of stranded cotton for the cross stitches and one strand for the backstitches. Use a beading needle and matching thread to attach the seed beads.

3 To personalize the sampler and change the family name and date, use the letters and numbers charted on page 19, planning out the letters on the graph paper provided to ensure they fit the space. Backstitch the details on to your sampler.

4 When all the stitching is complete, sew on the buttons with white thread. Press the work, avoiding the buttons and mount and frame your sampler as desired.

Seed beads give the pretty little cross stitch hanging heart a three-dimensional look.

13

Home Sweet Home Hanger

Stitch count of motif
10 high x 66 wide

Finished size
2 x 12cm (¾ x 4¾in)

You will need
- 14-count white Aida 12.5 x 23cm (5 x 9in)
- DMC stranded cotton (floss) as listed in chart key
- DMC Desire cord in purple
- Tapestry needle size 24–26
- Sheet of white card
- Pink patterned paper and pastel striped paper
- Two pale blue eyelets
- Medium-sized beads in pink, purple, mauve and white
- Two chipboard flowers
- Sticky-backed foam pads
- Scraps of ribbon
- Tiny pearl
- Double-sided adhesive tape or fabric glue

1 Stitch from the centre of the fabric and chart on page 16, cross stitching the words over one block of Aida using two strands of stranded cotton. Trim the fabric down to within two Aida blocks all round and back it with white card, using double-sided tape or glue.

2 Cut a piece of white card 6 x 14cm (2½ x 5½in) as the base of the hanger and cover the front with pink patterned paper. Fix two strips of pastel paper at the bottom of the card. Fix the cross stitch design above these strips.

3 Use a hole punch to punch two holes in the card hanger and set an eyelet in each. Thread the purple cord through one eyelet hole and wind it around itself to secure. Thread on beads and tie on ribbon scraps and then thread the cord through the other eyelet and wind round to secure.

4 Add the two chipboard flowers using foam pads and glue a pearl in the centre of the top flower to finish.

15

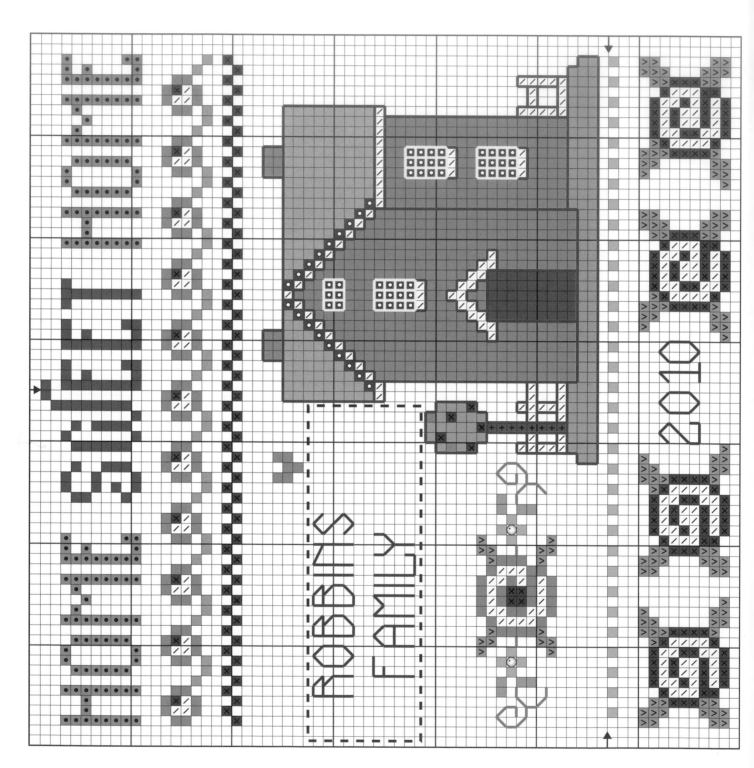

Home Sweet Home

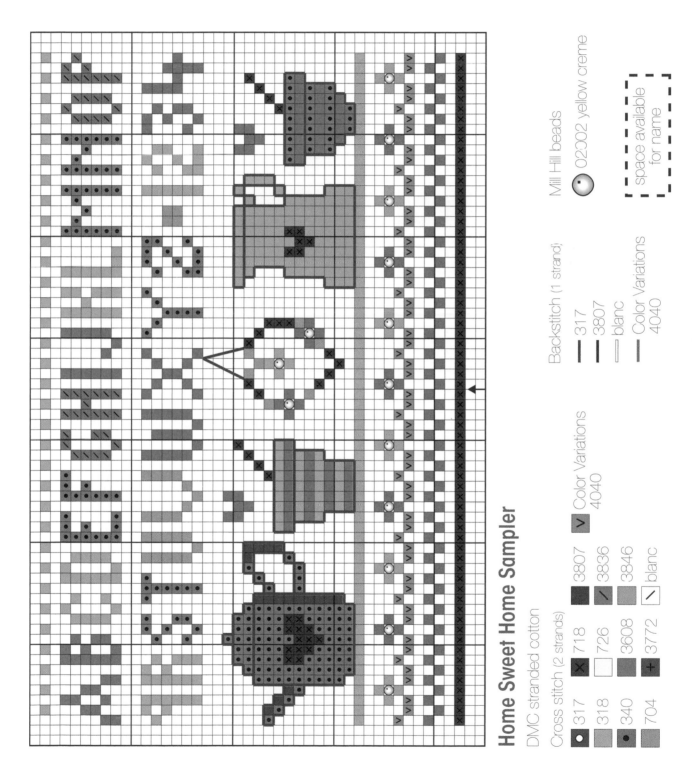

Home Sweet Home Sampler

DMC stranded cotton

Cross stitch (2 strands)

317 ⊙	718 ✗	726 □	340 ●	704 ▧
318 ▨		3608 ▦	3772 +	blanc ▨
3807 ▨	3836 ◹	3846 ▨	blanc ⧄	3807 V Color Variations 4040

Backstitch (1 strand)

— 317
— 3807
— blanc
— Color Variations 4040

Mill Hill beads

⊙ 02302 yellow creme

space available for name

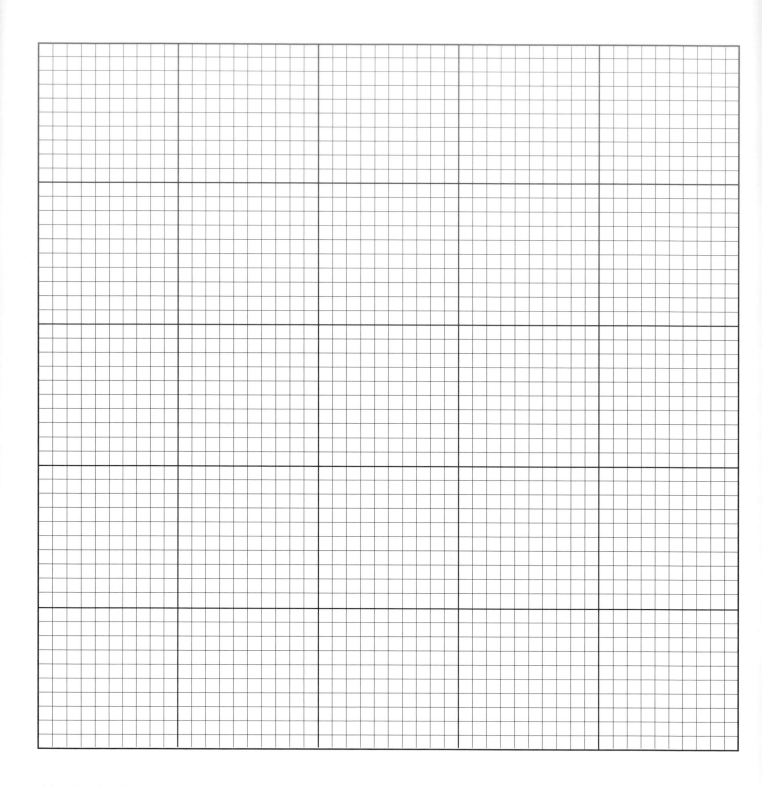

Use this blank grid to plan out the name and date for your sampler.
Use the letters and numbers charted opposite and work in pencil.
Remember to include spaces between the letters.

Home Sweet Home

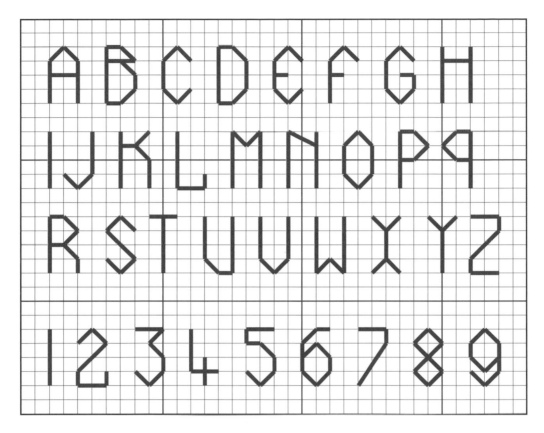

Home Sweet Home Alphabet

Use these letters and numbers to change the family name and the date on your sampler

Home is Where You
Hang Your Heart

2

Home is Where You Hang Your Heart

This sweet little sampler is very quick and easy to stitch. The design was inspired by the early naïve samplers of North America, showing a building, a flowering tree and some text, but has been given a modern twist with bright, fresh colours and a fun saying. For an extra special and unusual touch you could stitch the little heart motif on a separate piece of fabric as I have and turn it into a tiny stuffed heart to hang from a bright button.

A variation heart project, shown on page 26, makes a lovely decoration for the home. The heart could be hung on a hook or a door knob to brighten up any corner or would make a delightful house-warming gift. The chart on page 29 has lots of different hearts that you could use for your own small project ideas or use the whole chart to stitch a sampler.

Heart and home is the theme for both of the projects in this chapter. The stitching couldn't be easier — just whole cross stitch and a tiny amount of backstitch — but the results are utterly charming.

22

Home is Where You Hang Your Heart Sampler

1 Prepare your fabric for work and begin stitching in the centre of the fabric and from the centre of the chart on page 28.

2 Stitch over one block of Aida using two strands of stranded cotton for the cross stitches and one strand for the backstitches. If you are not making the stuffed heart you could cross stitch one of the little hearts from the chart on page 29 in its place. When all the stitching is complete press the work and mount and frame your sampler as desired.

3 If you wish to add a little stuffed heart, do so before framing, as follows. Stitch the heart from the chart on a square of 28-count white linen. Take a backing piece of the same linen and with right sides together sew round the heart shape. Trim excess fabric, make a small opening in the centre of the back and turn right side out. Press, stuff with polyester filling and sew up the opening. Sew the ribbon to the top and hang from the button.

Stitch count of motif
92 high x 80 wide

Finished size
16.7 x 14.5cm (6½ x 5¾in)

You will need
- 14-count pale pink Aida 26.5 x 25.5cm (10½ x 10in)
- DMC stranded cotton (floss) as listed in chart key
- Tapestry needle size 24–26

For the small stuffed heart (optional)
- Two 5cm (2in) squares of 28-count white linen
- One red button
- Polyester filling
- Narrow ribbon

A tiny little stuffed heart makes a lovely finishing touch to the sampler, or you could use it on a key ring instead.

Bright, fresh colours on pale pink Aida create a lovely effect, and Aida is so easy to stitch on.

25

 Home is Where You Hang Your Heart

1 The decoration shown uses the central motif from the chart on page 29 but the chart has lots of different hearts that could be used for other small projects or stitch the whole chart as a sampler. Prepare your fabric for work and begin stitching in the centre of the fabric and from the centre of the motif.

2 Stitch over one block of Aida using two strands of stranded cotton for the cross stitches. Press the work if necessary.

3 When stitching is complete make up the hanging as follows. Place the backing fabric and the stitched Aida right sides together, and using white sewing thread and a close running stitch, sew the fabrics together all around the edge of the shape.

4 Trim off excess fabric to within 6mm (¼in) of your stitched line all round. Make a slit in the backing fabric and turn the heart through to the right side. Stuff with polyester stuffing and sew up the slit in the back. Sew on the bluebird button and attach a loop of narrow ribbon for hanging.

Stuffed Heart Decoration

Stitch count of motif
53 high x 47 wide

Finished size
9.6 x 8.5cm (3¾ x 3½in)

You will need
- 14-count white Aida 13 x 13cm (5 x 5in)
- White backing fabric 13 x 13cm (5 x 5in)
- DMC stranded cotton (floss) as listed in chart key
- Tapestry needle size 24–26
- Polyester stuffing
- Narrow blue ribbon
- Tiny bluebird button (Just Another Button Company – see Suppliers)

Home is Where You Hang Your Heart Sampler

DMC stranded cotton

Cross stitch (2 strands)

				Backstitch (1 strand)
— 166	435	3765	✓ blanc	— 317
● 317	703	○ 3806		
341	725	3832		

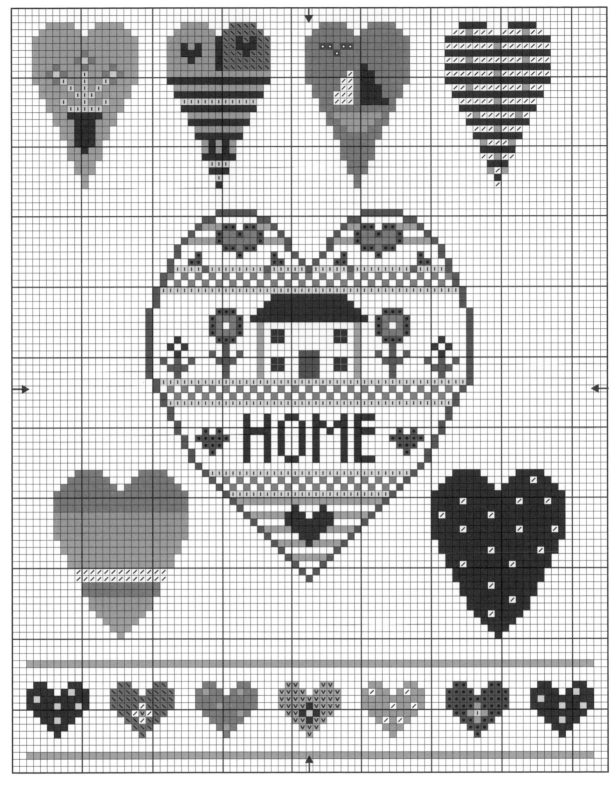

Hearts Sampler

DMC stranded cotton

Cross stitch (2 strands)

■ 310	■ 341	I 472	■ 996	■ 3851
● 317	■ 349	V 704	● 3607	/ blanc
＼ 340	■ 444	■ 995	■ 3608	

For the Stuffed Heart
Decoration stitch just
the central motif from
this chart

29

The Comforts of Home

3

The Comforts of Home

This soft and squashy cushion is comfortable to use and stylish to look at and would suit almost any décor. You can have fun embellishing your cushion with appliqué fabric flowers, as shown here created with bright modern fabrics, or add buttons of your choice if you prefer. The backing is made from a pretty, printed contemporary fabric with added button detailing, so the back of the cushion is also attractive to look at.

A second chunky square cushion on page 39 is a variation on the oblong cushion and is equally bright and inviting with a simple but effective cross stitch design and attractive embellishments. It is stitched in one colour, apart from the bees and flowers and could be made to exactly match the colour of your room. The back is made of two contrasting pieces of printed cotton. The two cushions make a great pair.

This wonderful cushion is stitched on a large count evenweave fabric so the cross stitch is quickly finished. The pretty appliqué flowers can be created from any print fabric and are edged with simple blanket stitch.

Oblong Home Cushion

1   Prepare your fabric for work and begin stitching in the centre of the fabric and from the centre of the chart on page 42.

2   Stitch over two threads of evenweave using three strands of stranded cotton for the cross stitches. Use two strands for the backstitch hanging bow on the letter O and one strand to outline the bees. Press the work.

3   When cross stitching is complete add the appliqué flowers as follows. Take your scraps of printed cottons and iron fusible web on to the back (according to the manufacturer's instructions). Cut out flower and leaf shapes with sharp scissors, either freehand or draw the shapes in pencil on the back of the fabrics.

4   Place the flowers and leaves on your cross stitch design until you are happy with the positions and then iron them to fuse in place. Using matching thread sew around each shape with blanket stitch (see page 105). See overleaf for making up the cushion.

Stitch count
47 high x 160 wide

Finished size
13.3 x 45cm (5¼ x 17¾in)

You will need
- 18-count white evenweave 60 x 35cm (24 x 14in), plus extra for seam allowances
- Two pieces of printed backing fabric for cushion cover, each 60 x 20cm (24 x 8in), plus extra for seam allowances
- DMC stranded cotton (floss) as listed in chart key
- Tapestry needle size 24–26
- Scraps of printed cottons to make appliqué flowers
- Fusible web (such as Bondaweb)
- Three coloured buttons for cushion back

Blanket stitch not only secures the appliqué edges but is a simple way to add an authentic homespun feel.

The Comforts of Home

Little details can make all the difference — whether it's some lovely hand stitching or some sweet fabric flowers.

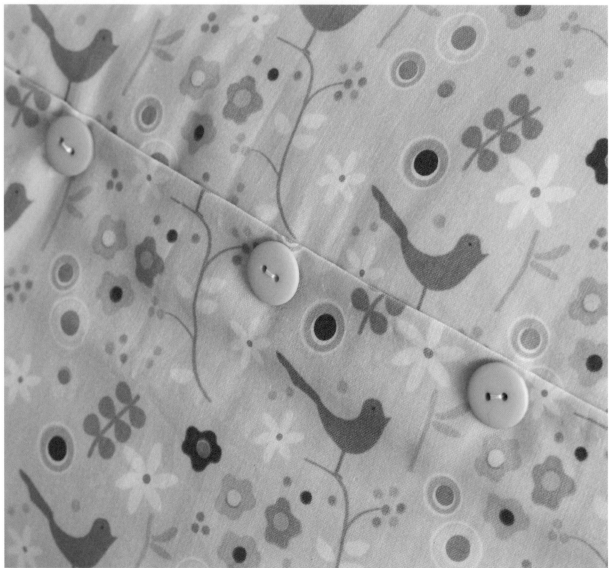

Making up the cushion

1 The cushion cover is an envelope type, where two pieces of backing fabric overlap at the centre of the cover along the length of the cushion. Begin by folding one long side of one of the backing fabric pieces in by 6mm (¼in) and hem. Press and place over the other piece of backing fabric, aligning edges all round, and pin in place.

2 Place the backing fabric pieces and the evenweave fabric right sides together and pin in place. Sew around all four sides of the cushion. Trim the seams and clip the corners to reduce bulk. Remove the pins holding the two back pieces together along the centre back.

3 Turn the cushion right way out and press the seams. Fold and arrange the back neatly and add some buttons for decoration along the fold line.

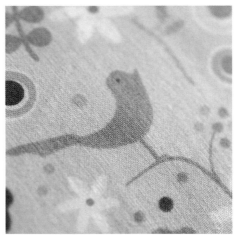

Cushion backs are the perfect place to experiment with patterned and unusual fabrics. When you want a change from the cross stitched side, just flip the cushion over for a burst of fun!

37

Square Home Cushion

Stitch count
88 high x 85 wide

Finished size
24.5 x 24cm (9¾ x 9½in)

You will need
- 18-count white evenweave fabric 40 x 40cm (15¾ x 15¾in) plus seam allowance
- DMC stranded cotton (floss) as listed in chart key
- Size 24–26 tapestry needle
- Printed cotton 12 x 12cm (4¾ x 4¾in) for the appliqué heart
- Fusible web (such as Bondaweb)
- Printed backing fabric, two different prints one 13 x 34cm (5 x 2½in) plus seam allowance, one 26 x 34cm (10¼ x 2½in) plus seam allowance
- Six coloured buttons
- Fabric scraps to make two yo-yos

1 Prepare your fabric for work and begin stitching in the centre of the fabric and from the centre of the chart on page 43.

2 Stitch over two fabric threads using three strands of stranded cotton for cross stitch and one strand for backstitch outlining around the bees.

3 When all the stitching is complete, take the printed fabric square for the heart appliqué and iron the fusible web on the back. Trace the heart template from page 40 on to the back of the fabric and cut out the shape.

4 Iron the appliqué heart in place on the front of the cushion next to the letter H, and sew around it in blanket stitch (see page 105) using matching thread.

5 Make a small yo-yo (see page 109) from pink fabric and sew to the appliqué heart, adding a green button in the centre. See overleaf for making up the cushion.

The Comforts of Home

Heart template (actual size)
for Square Home Cushion

Making up
the cushion

1 Fold the top of the largest piece of
backing fabric in to make a 1cm (⅜in)
hem. Fold the bottom edge of the contrasting
piece of backing fabric and make a 1cm (⅜in)
hem. Place the top backing piece over the lower
backing piece and pin in place.

2 Place the backing fabric and embroidered
evenweave fabric right sides together
and pin in place. Sew around all four sides of
the cushion. Trim the seam and clip the corners.
Remove the pins holding the two back pieces
together along the centre back.

3 Turn the right way out and press. Fold
the envelope back neatly and add some
buttons for decoration along the fold line. Make
a yo-yo from pink cotton fabric and stitch to
the backing on the right-hand side. Add a pink
button in the centre of the yo-yo to finish.

*Yo-yos are very easy to make and not
only add a splash of colour but also bring
an attractive three-dimensional quality.*

Buttons are great for
adding detail and texture,
and with so many colours
available you are sure to find
some to suit your fabric.

41

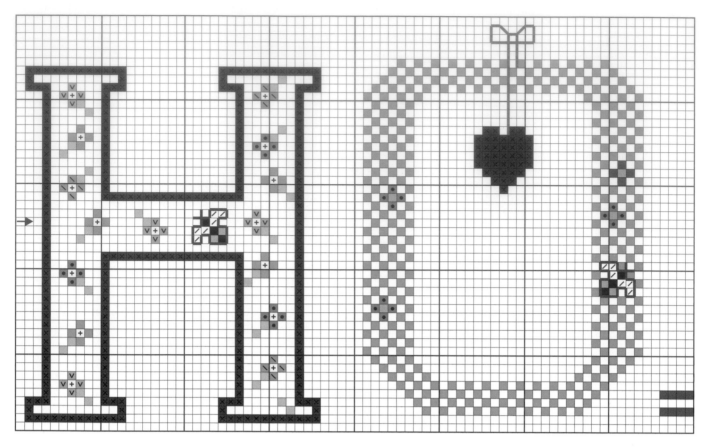

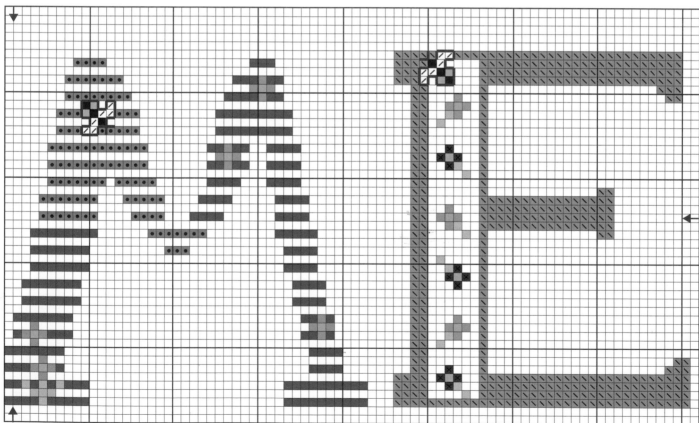

 The Comforts of Home

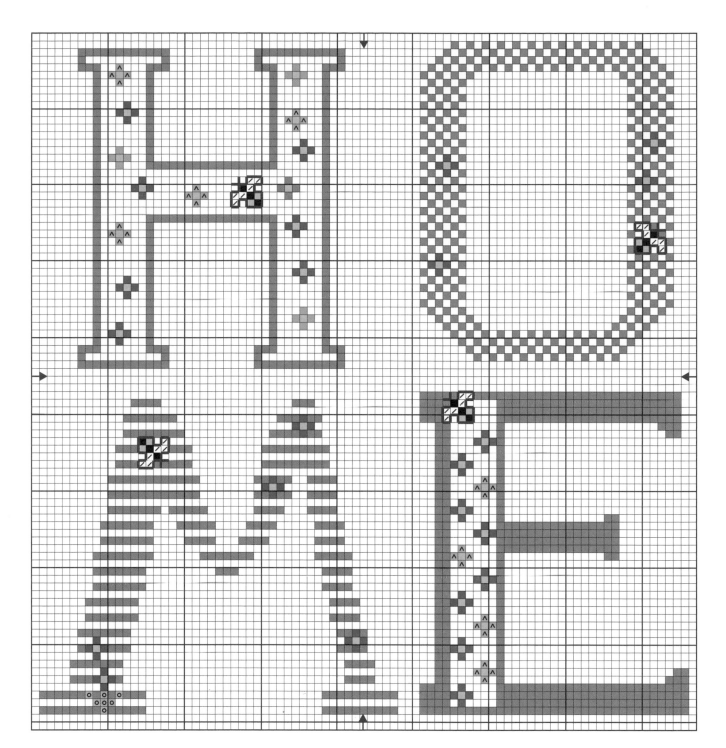

Oblong Home Cushion (left)

DMC stranded cotton

Cross stitch (2 strands)   Backstitch (1 strand)

■ 310	▨ 972	— 317
✕ 321	■ 996	— 3746
◣ 340	● 3607	
▨ 704	∨ 3608	
■ 718	◢ blanc	
+ 726		

Square Home Cushion (above)

DMC stranded cotton

Cross stitch (2 strands)

■ 310	■ 959	■ 996
∧ 604	■ 961	○ 3819
▨ 728	■ 995	◢ blanc

Backstitch (1 strand)
— 317

43

The Comforts of Home

La Maison Rouge

4

La Maison Rouge

Red and white samplers have been popular throughout sampler history, sometimes used to practise marking linen for future seamstresses and sometimes purely for decoration. There are many antique French samplers worked in red and white on beautiful old linen and their rich but faded colours and intricate techniques make them much sought after by collectors. My red and white home sampler shown here is a more contemporary take on the style, with ultra-white linen, a white frame and buttons. It has a contemporary look but the old French influences are still there.

A stylish greetings card on page 50 continues the red and white theme and is perfect for someone moving into a new home. The card is really easy to make and features a little cross stitched house, some bright card and rubber stamped lettering.

Using just one red shade of stranded cotton for the whole design, this sampler is so easy to stitch but makes such a wonderfully stylish statement.

Red and white make
a wonderfully crisp
colour combination.

La Maison Rouge Sampler

1 Prepare your fabric for work and begin stitching in the centre of the fabric and from the centre of the chart on pages 52/53.

2 Stitch over two threads of the linen using two strands of stranded cotton for the cross stitches and one strand for the backstitches. Use the numbers charted to change the date on your sampler.

3 When all the stitching is complete, sew on the buttons with either white or red thread to contrast. Press the work, avoiding the buttons and mount and frame your sampler as desired.

Stitch count of motif
198 high x 127 wide

Finished size
36 x 23cm (14 x 9in)

You will need
- 28-count white linen 45.5 x 33cm (18 x 13in)
- DMC stranded cotton (floss) as listed in chart key
- Tapestry needle size 24–26
- Eight buttons – six red and two white

Matching the frame to the fabric colour or the cross stitch shade creates a very modern look to a design.

 La Maison Rouge

1 Stitch from the centre of the fabric and use the little house motif at the top of the chart on page 52, cross stitching over two threads using two strands of stranded cotton.

2 When stitching is complete trim the fabric down to about 5.5 x 5cm (2 x 2¼in) and fray the edges of the fabric by four threads all round.

3 Using craft glue or double-sided tape, back the embroidery with thin white card. Put the stitching aside while you make the card.

4 Cut a white card blank 14.5 x 9cm (5¾ x 3½in). Cut a piece of red card 13.5 x 7cm (5¼ x 2¾in) and glue it to the centre of the white card front.

5 Glue the cross stitched house on to a piece of red card. Cut a piece of cream textured card 6.5 x 6cm (2½ x 2⅜in) and trim one edge with deckle-edged scissors. Attach the cross stitch motif to the cream card with red brads in the top corners and glue to the front of the card near the top.

6 Using rubber stamps and red ink, stamp out the New Home words on white card and then cut out to make letter tiles. Cut a tag 4 x 6cm (1½ x 2⅜in) from white or cream card and cover with the red gingham paper. Punch a hole in the top. Attach the letters to the tag using sticky pads and tie the ribbon through the hole. To finish, glue the tag to the card front about 1cm (⅜in) up from the bottom.

Red and White New Home Card

Stitch count of motif
15 high x 12 wide

Finished size
2.5 x 2.2cm (1 x ⅞in)

You will need
- 28-count white linen 7.5 x 7.5cm (3 x 3in)
- DMC stranded cotton (floss) as listed in chart key
- Tapestry needle size 24–26
- Thin white card to back embroidery
- Red and white card stock
- Cream textured card
- Red gingham paper
- Red and white brads
- Alphabet rubber stamps
- Red stamping ink
- Sticky-backed pads
- Cream ribbon
- Craft glue or double-sided tape

La Maison Rouge

La Maison Rouge
DMC stranded cotton
Cross stitch (2 strands)
■ 321

Backstitch (1 strand)
— 321

Use these charted
numbers to change
the date on your
sampler as desired

The Country Life

5

The Country Life

No crafter's home is complete without a sampler to welcome their friends and family and this chapter has two utterly charming little designs that suit that purpose perfectly. Welcome to Our House has a sweet little thatched country cottage and a beautiful garden of flowers. There are delicious strawberries in the border and two tiny white flower buttons for extra embellishment. The second sampler, Bless Our House, is just as delightful and full of country charm. It uses a favourite sampler saying and includes a lovely thatched cottage surrounded by trees, flowers and a white picket fence. The design is framed in a pretty heart-shaped mount.

If time is short the address book on page 62 has a sweet cottage that is very quick to stitch. With the addition of some charming buttons it would make a delightful gift for someone moving into a new house.

The two companion samplers in this chapter are a great pleasure to stitch. They feature pretty, country motifs in whole cross stitch with a little backstitch detailing and a delicate palette of country-garden colours. The addition of little buttons adds to the charm of these designs.

Welcome to Our House Sampler

Stitch count
84 high x 83 wide

Finished size
15.3 x 15.3cm (6 x 6in)

You will need
- 14-count Rustico Aida 25.5 x 25.5cm (10 x 10in)
- DMC stranded cotton (floss) as listed in chart key
- Tapestry needle size 24–26
- Two white flower buttons (Just Another Button Company 2279 – see Suppliers)

1   Prepare your fabric for work and begin stitching in the centre of the fabric and from the centre of the chart on page 64.

2   Stitch over one block of Aida using two strands of stranded cotton for the cross stitches except for the white (blanc) and the red (350) which use three strands. Use one strand for the backstitches.

3   When all the stitching is complete, sew on the buttons with yellow thread. Press the work, avoiding the buttons, and mount and frame your sampler as desired.

Pictorial buttons are great for these sort of samplers because you can match them to the sampler theme.

The Country Life

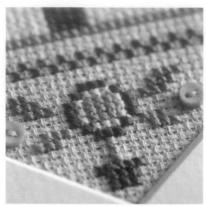

The designs in this chapter have many delightful little motifs that you could stitch for smaller projects.

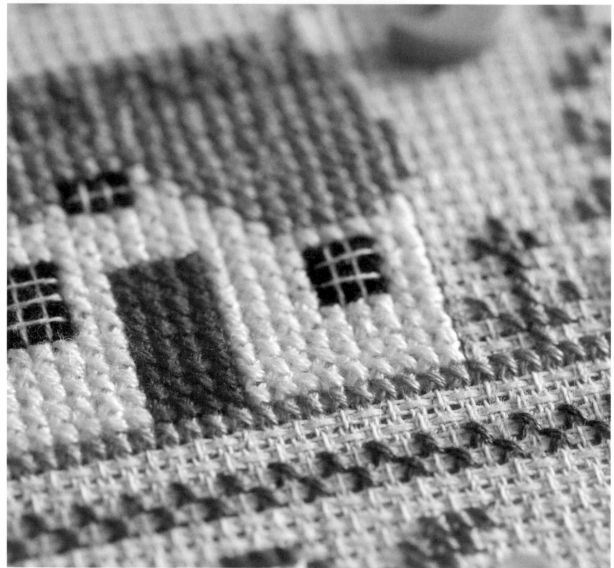

Bless Our House Sampler

Stitch count
69 high x 95 wide

Finished size
12.5 x 17.2cm (5 x 6¾in)

You will need
- 14-count Rustico Aida 23 x 28cm (9 x 11in)
- DMC stranded cotton (floss) as listed in chart key
- Tapestry needle size 24–26
- Two tiny pink buttons and one moon button (Just Another Button Company 3304 – see Suppliers)

1. Prepare your fabric for work and begin stitching in the centre of the fabric from the centre of the chart on page 65.

2. Stitch over one block of Aida using two strands of stranded cotton for the cross stitch. Use one strand for the backstitches except for the cottage roof detailing which uses two strands and long stitch.

3. When all the stitching is complete, sew on the buttons with matching thread. Press the work, avoiding the buttons, and mount and frame your sampler as desired.

A moon button adds a splash of colour but you could also use a little bird button.

61

The Country Life

Cottage Address Book

Stitch count of motif
25 high x 27 wide

Finished size
4.5 x 5cm (1¾ x 2in)

You will need
- 14-count Rustico Aida 10 x 10cm (4 x 4in)
- DMC stranded cotton (floss) as listed in chart key
- Tapestry needle size 24–26
- Fabric-covered or paper-covered address book
- White flower button and bluebird button (Just Another Button Company – see Suppliers)
- White card for backing
- Double-sided adhesive tape

1 Prepare your fabric for work and begin stitching in the centre of the fabric from the centre of the little chart on page 64.

2 Stitch over one block of Aida using two strands of stranded cotton for the cross stitches and one strand for the backstitches. When all the stitching is complete cut out the motif two holes away from the stitching all the way around.

3 Sew on the little buttons, with the white flower in the top right corner and the bluebird in the bottom left corner.

4 Using double-sided tape back the Aida with white card and attach the cottage motif to the front of your address book.

The Country Life

Welcome to Our House

DMC stranded cotton
Cross stitch (2 strands)

310
350 (3 strands)
434
553
702
841
907
972
3607
3851
3852
blanc (3 strands)

Backstitch
(1 strand)
— 317
— blanc

Address Book

DMC stranded cotton
Cross stitch (2 strands)

310
436
3328
3835
blanc

Backstitch (1 strand)
— 317
— blanc

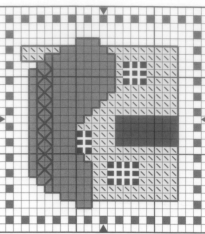

Bless Our House

DMC stranded cotton

Cross stitch

(2 strands)

■	310
I	434
●	437
■	703
V	704
■	742
■	792
/	3608
■	3805
/	blanc

Backstitch

(1 strand)

—— blanc

—— 317

(use two strands and long stitch for the roof detail)

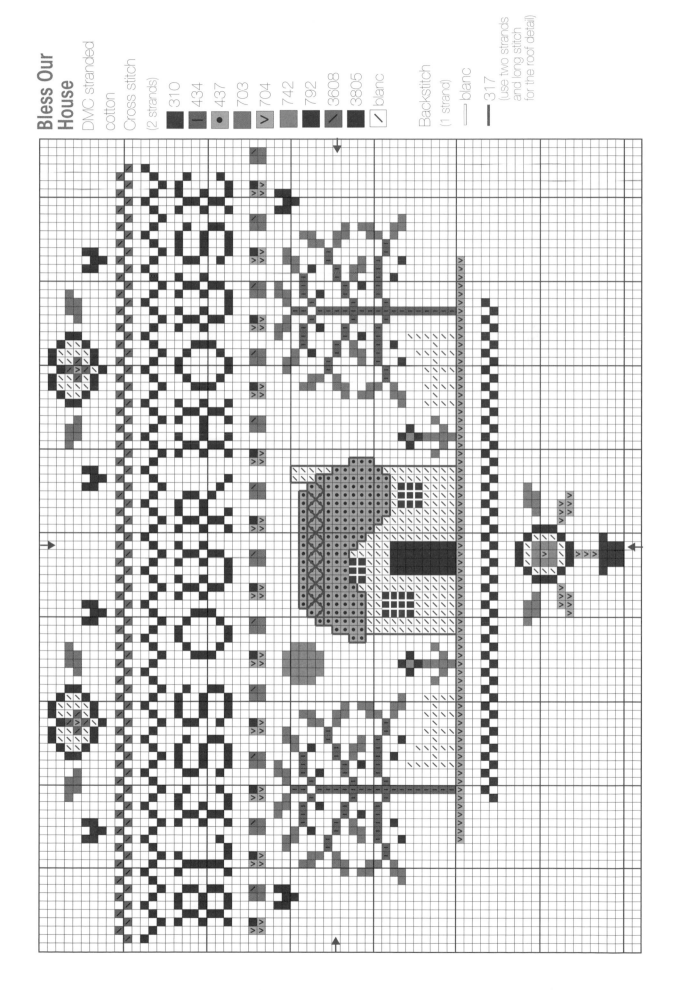

HEART OF THE HOME

6

Kitchen Comforts

This utterly charming kitchen-themed sampler has been made up as a little wall hanging to decorate the kitchen – the heart of your home. It hangs from a little wooden hanger with a cut-out heart, which has been painted pastel pink. You could use this idea, perhaps painting a plain wooden hanger to match your kitchen, or choosing one of the many wirework hangers available.

For some really quick projects that would make lovely gifts for friends and family you could stitch small motifs from the main sampler to make little jar covers, as shown on page 75, and fill them either with jams or preserves or collections of useful sewing knick-knacks. The cross stitch is worked on to printed cottons using waste canvas.

This little wall hanging is full of rustic charm and it would be very easy to change the colour of the fabric binding and the hanger to suit your kitchen.

HEART of THE HOME

Stitch count

83 high x 60 wide

Finished size

15 x 11cm (6 x 4¼in)

You will need

- 28-count antique white linen 25.5 x 20.3cm (10 x 8in)
- DMC stranded cotton (floss) as listed in chart key
- Printed cotton for backing 15 x 21cm (6 x 8¼in)
- Wadding (batting) 15 x 21cm (6 x 8¼in)
- White sewing thread for simple quilting
- Pink bias binding 2cm (¾in) wide x 1m (1yd) long
- One heart-shaped button

Heart of the Home Hanger

1 Prepare your fabric for work and begin stitching in the centre of the fabric and from the centre of the chart on pages 76/77.

2 Stitch over two threads of linen using two strands of stranded cotton for the full and three-quarter cross stitches and one strand for the backstitches.

3 When all the stitching is complete, press the design carefully and make up as a quilted hanger as described overleaf.

You could change the wording on this sampler using the backstitch alphabet charted on page 19.

70

You could use some of the little motifs to create small pictures in matching frames — perfect to decorate kitchen walls or shelves.

heart of THE HOME

Kitchen Comforts

Making up the hanger

1 Trim the linen fabric down to 15 x 21cm (6 x 8¼in) to match the backing fabric piece. Place the backing fabric on a work surface, right side down and put the wadding on top. Add the stitching, right side up. Use pins to hold this three-layer sandwich in place.

2 Using white sewing cotton, quilt with a running stitch around the cross stitch rectangles, around the lacy border and along the outside edge.

3 Bind the edges of the hanging with bias binding, as follows. Measure the outside edge of the hanging all round and cut binding long enough to go all the way round with 5cm (2in) extra for joining the ends. With right sides together, pin the binding to the edge all the way round. Tack (baste) the binding in place and remove the pins. Sew all round the edge of the binding by hand or machine.

4 Turn the binding over the raw edges and pin in place on the back of the hanging. Slipstitch neatly in place on the back, joining the ends at the top centre. Sew on a button to hide the join. Attach two pieces of bias binding to either side of the top to thread the hanger through.

Lines of white quilting secure all the layers together and also add a nice padded look to the design.

Preserve Jar Covers

Stitch count
13 high x 13 wide each

Finished size
2.5 x 2.5cm (1 x 1in) each

You will need
- Small pieces of 14-count waste canvas
- Small pieces of printed cottons in red, yellow and green
- DMC stranded cotton (floss) as listed in chart keys
- Tapestry needle size 24–26
- Fabric-covered elastic bands to fasten the covers

1 These instructions are for one cover but all three are made in the same way. Use pinking shears to cut an 18cm (7in) circle of printed cotton fabric. Find the centre of the circle and tack (baste) on a small piece of waste canvas larger than the cross stitch area.

2 Stitch the jar and lemon motifs from the main chart on page 76 and use the separate chart on page 77 for the cherries. Starting from the centre of the waste canvas and the centre of the charted motif, work the cross stitch over one block of the canvas using two strands of stranded cotton for cross stitches and one for backstitches.

3 When all stitching is complete, remove the tacking (basting) stitches and damp the waste canvas to soften the glue on its threads. Carefully withdraw the threads from behind the stitching using tweezers if necessary.

4 When all the waste canvas has been removed, press the jar cover and place it on top of the jar, using the elastic band to secure it.

Kitchen Comforts

Kitchen Comforts

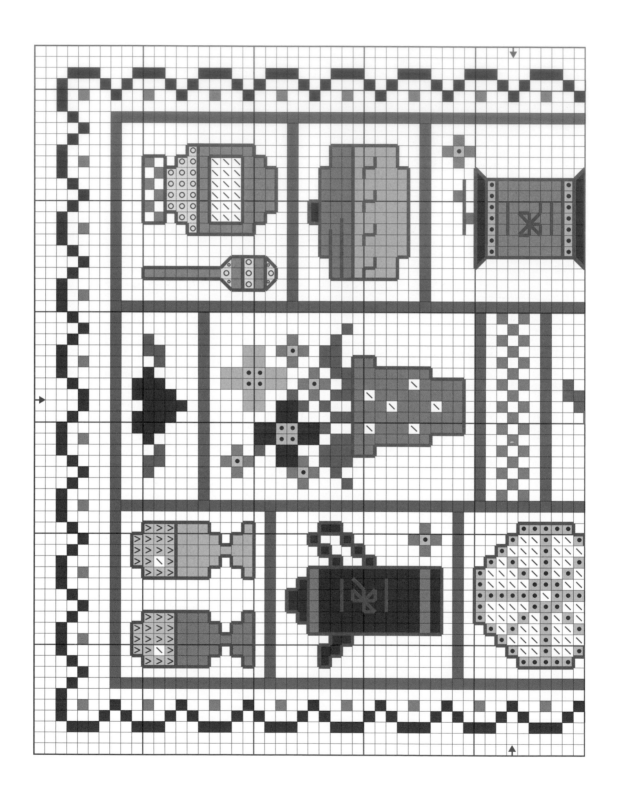

  Kitchen Comforts

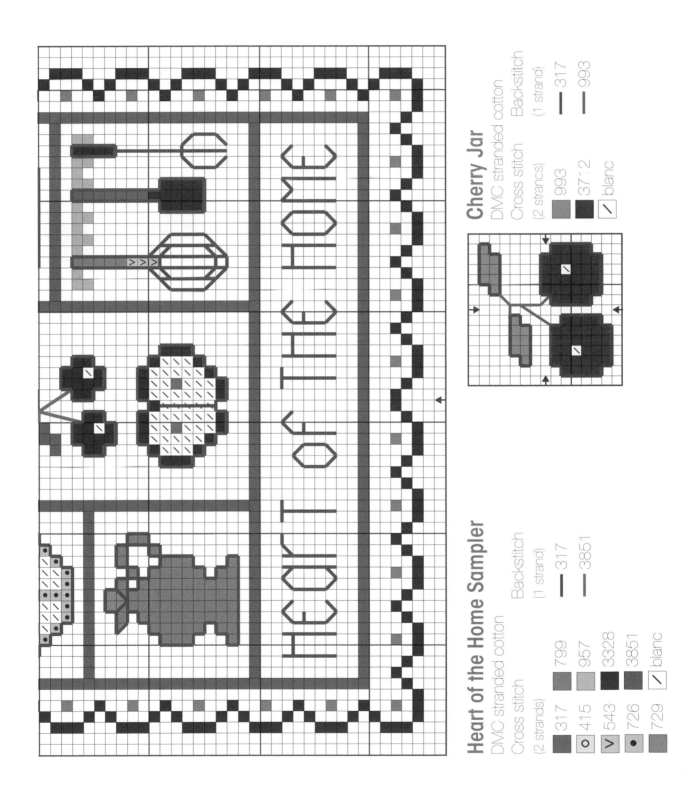

Cherry Jar

DMC stranded cotton

Cross stitch		Backstitch
(2 strands)		(1 strand)
993		— 317
371 2		— 993
☐ blanc		

Heart of the Home Sampler

DMC stranded cotton

Cross stitch		Backstitch
(2 strands)		(1 strand)
317	799	— 317
○ 415	957	— 3851
V 543	3328	
● 726	3851	
729	☐ blanc	

Home is Where
the Heart Is

7

Home is Where the Heart Is

The pretty sampler in this chapter is stitched on antique white linen and features a collection of darling little houses in gorgeous candy colours, each with its own flowers, topiary trees and pots. A bright chequerboard border and a row of colourful flowers complete the design, which is mounted in a simple white frame.

The little houses are also perfect to stitch individually for all kinds of projects and they have been used on pages 85–88 to create a charming little sewing set of pincushion, needle case and scissor keeper, which you could give as a gift or keep as a treat for yourself. The houses are stitched and mounted as patches on funky floral fabrics, with cute little buttons added for extra embellishment.

This fresh design couldn't be simpler to stitch — just whole cross stitch, backstitch and a couple of French knots. The mount and frame are plain and simple, giving a fresh, contemporary feel.

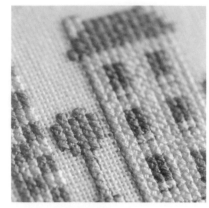

The delicious candy colours used in this design are so pretty and would brighten up any room.

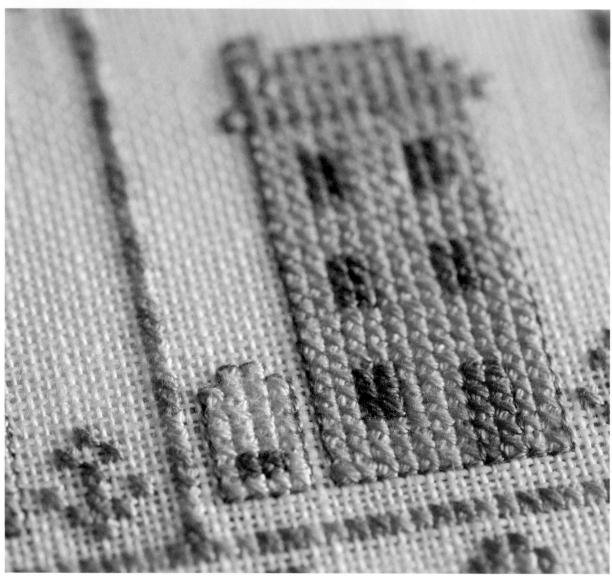

Home is Where the Heart Is

Home Is
Where the Heart
Is Sampler

Stitch count
96 high x 86 wide

Finished size
17.5 x 15.5cm (6¾ x 6¼in)

You will need
- 28-count antique white linen 28 x 25.4cm (11 x 10in)
- DMC stranded cotton (floss) as listed in chart key
- Size 24–26 tapestry needle

1. Prepare your fabric for work and begin stitching in the centre of the fabric from the centre of the chart on page 89.

2. Stitch over two threads of linen, using two strands of stranded cotton for the cross stitches, one strand for French knots and one strand for the backstitches.

3. When all the stitching is complete, press your work carefully and frame as a picture.

Instead of stitching the heart motif you could sew on a heart-shaped button instead.

 Home is Where the Heart Is

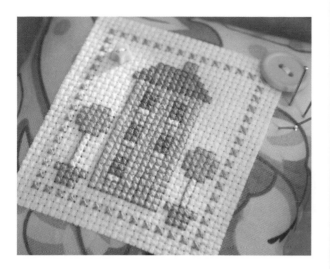

1 Prepare your fabric for work and begin stitching the house motif in the centre of the fabric from the centre of the motif on the chart on page 89.

2 Stitch over one block of Aida, using two strands of stranded cotton for cross stitches and one strand for backstitches. Stitch a row of alternate dark pink cross stitches around the motif.

3 When the stitching is complete, trim the Aida down to three holes away from the stitching all the way round. Iron a piece of fusible web on to the back.

4 Take the two pieces of printed cotton and with right sides together sew all the way round leaving a small gap for turning through. Trim seams, clip corners and turn right side out. Press and then iron the cross stitch house motif to the front of the pincushion, fusing it to the fabric.

5 Sew on the buttons with matching thread. Stuff the pincushion with polyester filling and slipstitch the gap closed to finish.

Little House Pincushion

Stitch count of motif
31 high x 27 wide

Finished size
5.8 x 5cm (2¼ x 2in)

You will need
- 14-count white Aida 10 x 10cm (4 x 4in)
- DMC stranded cotton (floss) as listed in chart key
- Tapestry needle size 24–26
- Two pieces of printed cotton fabric 11 x 11cm (4¼ x 4¼in) plus seam allowance
- Fusible web (such as Bondaweb)
- Polyester stuffing
- Two decorative buttons

Little House Needle Case

Stitch count of motif
31 high x 27 wide

Finished size
5.8 x 5cm (2¼ x 2in)

You will need
- 14-count white Aida 10 x 10cm (4 x 4in)
- DMC stranded cotton (floss) as listed in chart key
- Tapestry needle size 24–26
- Two different printed cotton fabrics 22 x 11cm (8½ x 4¼in) plus seam allowance
- Fusible web (such as Bondaweb)
- Pale green felt 19 x 8cm (7½ x 3in), trimmed with pinking shears
- Two decorative buttons

1 Prepare your fabric for work and begin stitching the house motif in the centre of the fabric from the centre of the motif on the chart on page 89.

2 Stitch over one block of Aida, using two strands of stranded cotton for cross stitches and one strand for backstitches. Stitch a row of alternate dark pink cross stitches around the motif.

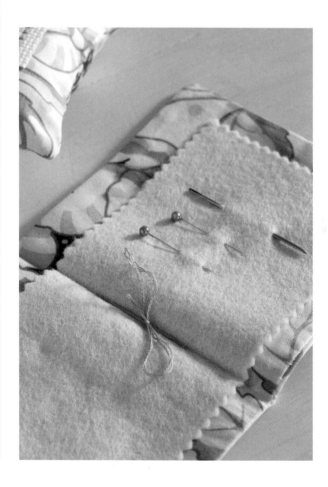

Home is Where the Heart Is

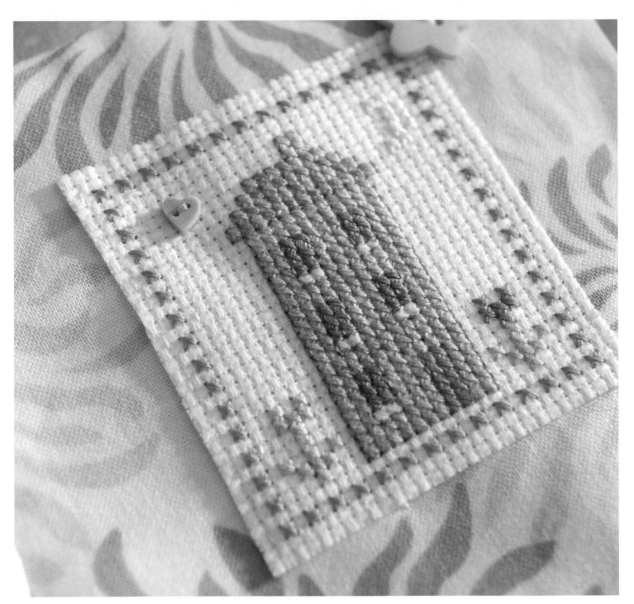

3 When the stitching is complete, trim the Aida down to two holes away from the stitching all the way round. Iron a piece of fusible web on to the back.

4 Take the two pieces of printed cotton and with right sides together sew all the way round leaving a small gap for turning through. Trim seams, clip corners, turn right side out and slipstitch the gap closed. Press and then iron the cross stitch house motif to the front of the needle case, fusing it to the fabric. Sew on the buttons with matching thread.

5 Fold the piece of felt in half and place it inside the needle case. Using three strands of pink cotton, make a big running stitch along the fold to secure the two layers together. Tie the thread in a bow on the inside of the needle case to finish.

Little House Scissor Keeper

1 Prepare your fabric for work and begin stitching the house in the centre of the fabric from the centre of the motif on the chart opposite. Omit the trees either side of the house.

2 Stitch over two threads of linen, using two strands of stranded cotton for cross stitches and one strand for backstitches. Stitch a row of alternate dark pink cross stitches around the motif.

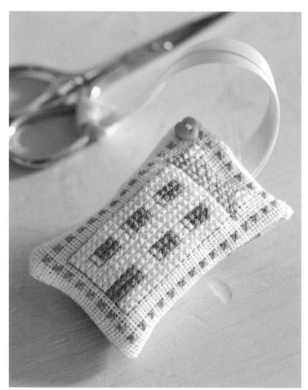

Stitch count of motif
29 high x 17 wide

Finished size
5 x 3cm (2 x 1¼in)

You will need
- 28-count white linen 10 x 10cm (4 x 4in)
- DMC stranded cotton (floss) as listed in chart key
- Tapestry needle size 24–26
- Small piece of printed cotton fabric for backing
- Polyester filling
- Narrow green ribbon
- Two decorative buttons

3 When the stitching is complete trim 1cm (⅜in) away from the stitching all the way round. Take the piece of printed cotton backing fabric and cut it to the same size as the embroidered linen. Place it right sides together with the linen and sew around three sides, leaving the top open for stuffing. Trim seams, clip corners and turn right side out.

4 Press the scissor keeper and stuff with polyester filling. Sew up the opening and then sew on one of the decorative buttons with matching thread. Fold the ribbon in half and sew to the top of the scissor keeper at the back, hiding the stitches with a tiny button.

Home is Where the Heart Is

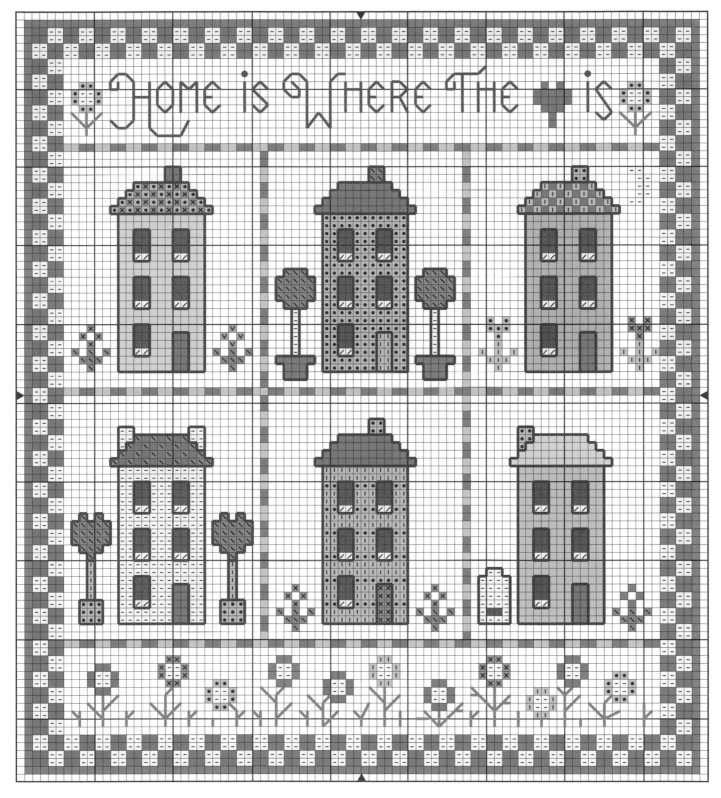

Home is Where the Heart is

DMC stranded cotton

Cross stitch (2 strands)

- 153
- 317
- 605
- 827
- / ecru
- 166
- × 340
- − 727
- \ 907
- V 209
- I 598
- 799
- 3608

Backstitch (1 strand)

— 317
— 907
— 3807

French knots (1 strand)

● 3807

8

A Christmas Welcome

This sweet little seasonal sampler is a cosy celebration of the delights of home at Christmas time. The little house nestling in the snowy hills has welcoming smoke coming from the chimney and all the lights are on to greet the family as they arrive home. The folk-art style of this sampler would suit almost any room and would look particularly attractive in a festively decorated hall or sitting room.

Two of the motifs from the main design have been used to create the smaller projects shown on pages 96 and 99. The lovely little snowy cottage card is in a shabby-chic style, perfect to accompany the sampler if you are giving it as a gift, while a gift tag full of hearts is the perfect way to send your love at Christmas time.

Full of charming little motifs all gathered together in a beautifully coloured design, this sampler is easy to stitch. The raw linen it is stitched on and the distressed frame give it a lovely antique feel.

All Hearts Come Home for Christmas

Stitch count
76 high x 76 wide

Finished size
13.8 x 13.8cm (5½ x 5½in)

You will need
- 28-count raw linen 24 x 24cm (9½ x 9½in)
- DMC stranded cotton (floss) as listed in chart key
- Size 24–26 tapestry needle

1 Prepare your fabric for work and begin stitching in the centre of the fabric from the centre of the chart on page 100.

2 Stitch over two threads of the linen, using two strands of stranded cotton for the full and three-quarter cross stitches, one strand for French knots and one strand for backstitches.

3 When all the stitching is complete, press your work carefully and frame as a picture.

The charming little motifs that make up this festive sampler design are perfect to create small gifts.

The subtle, antique colouring of this sampler will stand the test of time and be a Christmas favourite for years to come.

A Christmas Welcome

Snowy Cottage Card

Stitch count
26 high x 34 wide

Finished size
4.7 x 6.2cm (1⅞ x 2½in)

You will need
- 14-count Aida in natural 10 x 11.5cm (4 x 4½in)
- DMC stranded cotton (floss) as listed in chart key
- Tapestry needle size 24–26
- Sheet of cream card
- Cream card blank 10 x 13cm (4 x 5in)
- Four brown photo corners
- Strip of red spotty fabric or paper
- Rubber stamps for the message
- Fabric glue or double-sided adhesive tape

1 Prepare your fabric for work and begin stitching in the centre of the fabric from the centre of the chart on page 101.

2 Stitch over one block of Aida, using two strands of stranded cotton for cross stitches.

3 When all the stitching is complete, press the design and back it with cream card using fabric glue or double-sided tape. Add a photo corner to each corner of the little design and tape in place at the back.

4 Take the cream card blank and attach the strip of spotty fabric or paper near the bottom. Attach the cross stitch design to the top of the card, and then create a little message on a small piece of cream card using rubber stamps. Attach this on an angle in the bottom right corner.

All Hearts Gift Tag

Stitch count
18 high x 42 wide

Finished size
3.3 x 7.6cm (1¼ x 3in)

You will need
- 14-count Aida in natural 7.5 x 13cm (3 x 5in)
- DMC stranded cotton (floss) as listed in chart key
- Tapestry needle size 24–26
- Pinking shears
- Cream card or felt
- Raffia

1 Prepare your fabric for work and begin stitching in the centre of the fabric from the centre of the chart on page 101.

2 Stitch over one block of Aida, using two strands of stranded cotton for cross stitches.

3 When all the stitching is complete, press the design and cut out three holes away from the stitching all the way round using pinking shears.

4 Take a piece of cream card or felt and place behind the tag. Pierce a hole in the top centre and tie together with raffia.

All Hearts Come Home for Christmas

DMC stranded cotton

Cross stitch (2 strands)

■ 223	V 352	■ 931	⊙ 3854
■ 310	502	3052	/ ecru
− 318	● 680	■ 3726	

Backstitch (1 strand)

— 310
— 317
— 3052
— 3854

French knots (1 strand)

● 310

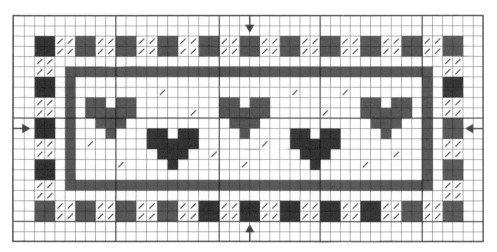

All Hearts Gift Tag

DMC stranded cotton

Cross stitch (2 strands)

- ■ 223
- ■ 3726
- ☑ ecru

Snowy Cottage Card

DMC stranded cotton

Cross stitch (2 strands)

■ 223	■ 3726	
■ 310	◯ 3854	
▬ 318	☑ ecru	

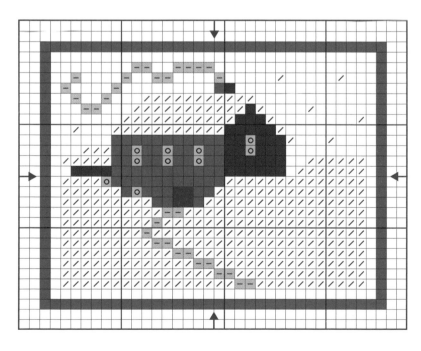

Materials, Techniques and Making Up

This section should be particularly useful to beginners as it contains information on the materials and equipment you will need and the basic techniques needed to work the projects in the book. Refer to Suppliers for useful addresses.

Materials

Fabrics

The designs have been worked on a blockweave fabric called Aida and on evenweave or linen fabrics. If working on Aida, stitch over one block; if working on evenweave stitch over two fabric threads. If you change the gauge (the count) of the material, that is the number of holes per inch, then the size of the finished work will alter accordingly. See opposite for working out stitch counts and design sizes.

Waste Canvas

This material is designed for stitching on fabrics where cross stitching wouldn't normally be possible because the threads are uneven or very tightly woven, for example clothing. It is used to cross stitch on printed fabric for the preserve jars on page 75.

Needles

Tapestry needles, available in different sizes, are used for cross stitch as they have a rounded point and therefore do not snag the fabric. A few of the projects use glass seed beads for extra sparkle and dimension and you will need a thinner beading needle to attach these.

Threads

The projects have been stitched with DMC stranded embroidery cotton (floss) but you could match the colours to other thread ranges – ask at your local needlework store. The six-stranded skeins can easily be split into separate strands. The project instructions and charts tell you how many strands to use. Some projects use DMC Color Variations threads, which are variegated threads. Use these in the same way as stranded cotton.

Frames

It is a matter of personal preference as to whether you use an embroidery frame to keep your fabric taut while stitching. Generally speaking, working with a frame helps to keep the tension even and prevent distortion, while working without a frame is faster and less cumbersome. There are various types on the market – look in your local needlework store for some examples.

Techniques

Stitch Count and Design Size

The majority of the charts in this book are worked on 14-count Aida or 28-count linen or evenweave fabric. You can stitch the designs on fabric with a lower or higher count than this, as long as you are aware that it will change the finished size of the design. Being able to calculate the eventual size of a design means that you can decide how much fabric you need for a particular project or whether a design will fit a specific picture frame or card aperture.

To work out the stitch count, first count how many stitches there are along the height of a design and then along the width – this is called the stitch count (don't forget to count backstitches and French knots too on the outer edge of a design). These stitch counts are provided with each project in this book. To work out a finished design size yourself, divide each of the stitch count numbers by the fabric count of the embroidery fabric you want to use. For example, a charted design 140 stitches high x 112 stitches wide worked on 14-count Aida fabric would be 140 ÷ 14 = 10in (25.5cm) and 112 ÷ 14 = 8in (20.3cm). So the finished design would be 10 x 8in (25.5 x 20.3cm).

When calculating design sizes for evenweave fabrics, divide the fabric count by 2 before you start, because evenweave is worked over two threads not one block as with Aida.

Preparing the Fabric

Spending some time preparing embroidery fabric before stitching will save time in the long run.

• Before starting work, check the design size given with each project and make sure that this is the size you require for your finished embroidery. Your fabric must be larger than the finished design size to allow for making up, so allow 10cm (4in) to both dimensions when stitching a sampler and 5cm (2in) for smaller projects.

• Before beginning to stitch, neaten the fabric edges either by hemming or zigzagg stitching to prevent fraying as you work. Use pinking shears can help.

• Find the centre of the fabric. This is important regardless of which direction you work from, in order to stitch the design centrally on the fabric. To find the centre, fold the fabric in half horizontally and then vertically, then tack (baste) along the folds (or use tailor's chalk). The centre point is where the two lines of tacking meet. This point on the fabric should correspond to the centre point on the chart. Remove these lines on completion of the work.

Using Charts and Keys

The charts in this book are easy to work from. Each square represents one stitch. Each coloured square, or coloured square with a symbol, represents a thread colour, with the code number given in the chart key. A few of the designs use fractional stitches (three-quarter cross stitches) to give more definition. Solid coloured lines show where backstitches or long stitches are to be worked. French knots are shown by coloured circles. Larger coloured circles with a dot indicate beads. Each complete chart has arrows at the side to show the centre point, which you could mark with a pen.

Caring for Finished Work

Cross stitch embroidery can be washed and ironed, though care should be taken with delicate ceramic buttons. Make sure it is colourfast first, then wash with bleach-free soap in hand-hot water, squeezing gently but never rubbing or wringing. Rinse in cold or lukewarm water and dry naturally.

To iron cross stitch embroidery, use a hot setting on a steam iron. Cover the ironing board with thick towels and place the stitching on this, right side down. Press the fabric firmly but avoid charms, buttons or metallic threads.

103

Stitches

Starting and Finishing

It is always a good idea to start and finish work correctly, to create the neatest effect and avoid ugly bumps and threads trailing across the back of work. To finish off thread, pass the needle through several nearby stitches on the wrong side of the work, then cut the thread off, close to the fabric.

Knotless Loop Start Starting this way can be very useful with stranded cotton (floss), but only works if you are intending to stitch with an even number of threads, i.e. 2, 4 or 6. Cut the stranded cotton roughly twice the length you would normally need and separate out one strand. Double this strand and thread your needle with the two ends. Pierce your fabric from the wrong side where you intend to place your first stitch, leaving the looped end at the back of the work. Return your needle to the wrong side after forming a half cross stitch and pass the needle through the waiting loop. Pull the loop snugly. You can now begin to stitch.

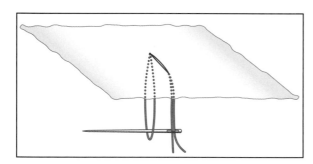

Fig 1 Beginning stitching with a knotless loop

Away Waste Knot Start Start this way if working with an odd number of strands or when using variegated threads. Thread your needle and make a knot at the end. Take the needle and thread through from the front of the fabric to the back and come up again about 2.5cm (1in) away from the knot. Now

either start cross stitching and work towards the knot, cutting it off when the threads are anchored, or thread the end into your needle and finish off under some completed stitches.

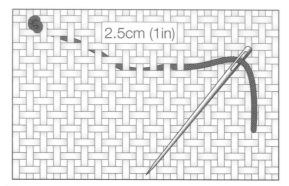

Fig 2 Beginning stitching with an away waste knot

Backstitch

Backstitch is indicated on the charts by a solid coloured line. It can be worked on its own for lettering, on top of other stitches for detail and as an outline around areas of completed cross stitches to add definition. Backstitch is normally worked with one strand of thread.

To work backstitch, bring the needle up through the fabric at 1 (see diagram below), then take it down at 2. Bring it back up at 3 and then down at 4. Repeat the process to make the next stitch. This produces short stitches at the front of the work and longer ones at the back.

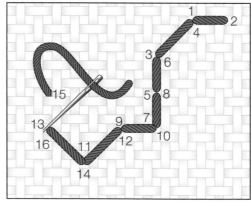

Fig 3 Working backstitch

Blanket Stitch

This stitch is used decoratively to edge appliqué motifs and can be spaced according to your preference. When very tightly spaced it is called buttonhole stitch.

To work blanket stitch, bring the needle and thread out at 1 as shown in the diagram below, insert it at 2 and then bring out at 3, keeping the thread *under* the needle and pulling the thread so that it lies snugly against the fabric without distortion. Continue in the same way, following the outline of the motif you are edging.

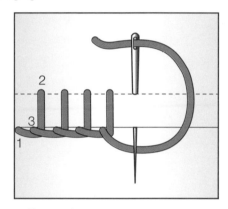

Fig 4 Working blanket stitch

Cross Stitch

This is the main stitch used throughout the projects and each complete cross stitch is represented on the charts by a coloured square. The cross stitches in this book are usually worked over two threads of evenweave (linen) or one block of Aida.

A cross stitch is worked in two stages: a diagonal stitch is worked over two threads (or one block), then a second diagonal stitch is worked over the first stitch in the opposite direction, forming a cross (see Figs 5a and 5b).

Fig 5a A single cross stitch on Aida

Fig 5b A single cross stitch on evenweave

If you have a large area to cover, you may prefer to work the cross stitches in two journeys, in rows. Work a row of half cross stitches in one direction, then work back in the opposite direction with the diagonal stitches needed to complete each cross stitch (see Figs 6a and 6b). The upper stitches of all the crosses should lie in the same direction to produce a neat effect.

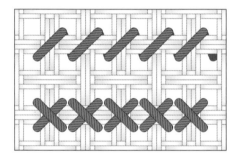

Fig 6a Cross stitch worked in two journeys on Aida

Fig 6b Cross stitch worked in two journeys on evenweave

Three-quarter Cross Stitch

This is a part or fractional stitch that is useful for adding detail to a design and creating smoother curves or circles. Three-quarter cross stitch is shown on the charts by a coloured triangle within a square.

To work three-quarter cross stitch, work a half cross stitch, then a quarter stitch in the opposite direction, bringing the needle down in the centre of the half cross stitch already worked (see diagram), piercing the centre of a block if working on Aida.

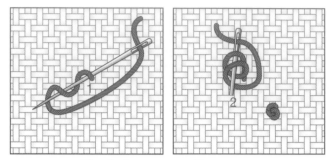

Fig 8 Working a French knot

Fig 7 Working three-quarter cross stitch

French Knot

This is a useful little stitch and may be used in addition to cross stitch to add texture and emphasis. In this book they are usually worked with two strands of thread wound once around the needle and are shown on the charts by a small coloured circle.

To work a French knot, bring the needle up to the right side of the fabric, hold the thread down with your left thumb (if right-handed) and wind the thread around the needle twice (see diagrams). Still holding the thread taut put the needle through to the back of the work, one thread or part of a block away from the entry point. If you want bigger knots, add more thread to the needle.

Attaching Beads

Attach beads using a beading needle or very fine 'sharp' needle. Use thread that matches the bead colour and secure with either a half cross stitch or a full cross stitch.

Materials, Techniques and Making Up

Tips for Perfect Stitching

Cross stitch is a simple stitch and easy to do but your work will look its best if you follow these guidelines.

- Wash your hands before beginning stitching, and use hand cream to keep them smooth.
- Always work in a good light, near a window during the day or with a special 'daylight' lamp at night.
- Use the knotless loop method (page 104) to start your stitching – it stops knots spoiling the surface of your work.
- If you stitch with variegated thread use an away waste knot start (page 104).
- Make sure that your cross stitches all have the top stitches facing in the same direction.
- Don't pull the thread too tight – be gentle and consistent and the result will be more professional.
- If you find it difficult to stitch accurately, use an embroidery hoop.
- To prevent thread becoming tangled, 'drop' the needle occasionally to allow the thread to untwist.
- Tidy your work away in a cotton bag, or if it is a large piece on a frame cover it with an old sheet to protect it from dust and marks.
- Sort your spare threads on bobbins and store neatly in boxes or drawers – it will save time when you search for specific threads later.

Making Up

Most of the samplers in this book have been framed as pictures or prepared as wall hangings, so advice on mounting and framing is given below. The smaller projects have been made up in various simple ways, described within the project instructions.

Using Iron-on Interfacing and Fusible Web

Iron-on interfacing can be used to stiffen and stabilize your cross stitch embroidery and allow the edges to be cut without fraying. Cut the interfacing to size and fuse it to the back of the finished embroidery with a medium-hot iron, placing the embroidery face down on some thick towels.

Fusible web allows you to fuse the embroidery to another fabric with a medium-hot iron. This means that you can also use your cross stitch to decorate all sorts of ready-made items.

Mounting and Framing Embroidery

It is best to take large samplers to a professional framer, where you can choose from a wide variety of mounts and frames that will best enhance your work. The framer will be able to lace and stretch the fabric correctly and cut mounts accurately.

If you intend to mount the work yourself, use acid-free mounting board in a colour that will not show through the embroidery. Cut the board to fit inside your picture frame and allow for the thickness of the fabric pulled over the edges of the board. There are two common methods used for mounting – taping and lacing

Taping Method Place the cut board on the reverse of the work in the position required. Starting from the centre of one of the longest edges, fold the fabric over the board and pin through the fabric into the edge of the board to keep the fabric from moving. Check it is in the correct place with no wrinkles or bumps, then stick the work in place using strips of double-sided adhesive tape, removing the pins once finished.

Lacing Method Pin the work in place on the board, as above, then working from the centre and using long lengths of strong thread, lace backwards and forwards across the gap. Repeat for the shorter sides, taking care to mitre or fold the corners in neatly. Remove pins once finished.

Mounting Work into Cards

Many of the samplers have smaller motifs that could be stitched and mounted into cards. There are many lovely card mounts available today. Double-fold cards are pre-folded with three sections, the middle one having a window for your embroidery.

Trim your design to the correct size – about 1.3cm (½in) larger than the aperture on all sides.

 Materials, Techniques and Making Up

Position double-sided tape around the window area and remove the tape backing. Lay the card on top of the embroidery so it shows neatly through the window and press into place. Fold the third of the card to cover the back of the embroidery and secure with more double-sided tape.

Making a Yo-yo

Yo-yos make attractive embellishments to cross stitch designs and have been used on the square cushion on page 39.

   To make a yo-yo start with a circle of fabric twice the size that you want the finished yo-yo to be. Fold the edges over all round by 6mm (¼in) and use strong sewing thread to make a running stitch all round this folded edge (see diagrams, right). Pull the thread up and gather the fabric so only a small gap remains. Secure the thread and press the yo-yo. The yo-yo can then be attached to a fabric base, gathered side up, with slipstitches. You could add a button, bead or some decorative stitches in the centre if you wish.

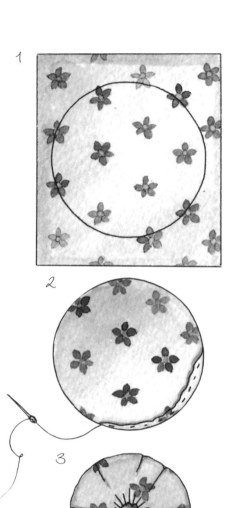

1

2

3

Making a Yo-Yo

109

Suppliers

UK

Debbie Cripps
8 Christchurch Street West, Frome,
Somerset BA11 1EQ
Tel: 01373 454448
www.debbiecripps.co.uk
For aperture boxes, beads, buttons and charms

Dee Fine Arts
182 Telegraph Road, Heswall, Wirral CH60 0AJ
Tel: 0151 342 6657
For expert embroidery and picture framing

DMC Creative World
1st Floor Compass Building, Feldspar Close,
Warren's park, Enderby, Leicestershire LE19 4SD
Tel: 0116 275 4000
www.dmccreative.co.uk
www.dmc-usa.com
*For stranded cottons, metallic threads, embroidery
fabrics and other supplies*

HobbyCraft Superstores
Help Desk, The Peel Centre, St Ann Way, Gloucester,
Gloucestershire GL1 5SF
Tel: 01452 424999
www.hobbycraft.co.uk
*For a huge range of craft supplies, including beads
(stores throughout the UK)*

Sew and So
Stroud House, Russell Street, Stroud, Glos GL5 3AN
Tel: 01453 889988
www.sewandso.co.uk
*For Just Another Button Company buttons, coloured
linen and threads*

Voirrey Embroidery Centre
Brimstage Hall, Wirral CH63 6JA
Tel: 0151 342 3514
www.voirryembroidery.co.uk
For embroidery supplies

USA

Charles Craft Inc.
PO Box 1049, Laurenburg, NC 28353
Tel: 910 844 3521
www.charlescraft.com
*For fabrics for cross stitch and many useful
pre-finished items*

The City Quilter
157 West 24th Street, New York, NY 1011
Tel: 212 807 0390
*For patchwork and quilting supplies
(shop and mail order)*

Joann Stores, Inc
5555 Darrow Road, Hudson, Ohio
Tel: 1 888 739 4120
www.joann.com
*For general needlework and quilting supplies
(mail order and shops across US)*

MCG Textiles
13845 Magnolia Avenue, Chino, CA 91710
Tel: 909 591-6351
www.mcgtextiles.com
For cross stitch fabrics and pre-finished items

Mill Hill, a division of Wichelt Imports Inc.
N162 Hwy 35, Stoddard WI 54658
Tel: 608 788 4600
www.millhill.com
For Mill Hill beads

www.superbuzzy.com
Useful website for fabrics and craft items

www.reprodepotfabric.com
Useful website for fabrics and craft items

Acknowledgments

Thank you to everyone at David & Charles for their bright ideas, hard work and skill in producing this book. Thank you to Cheryl Brown for commissioning the book and for all her ideas and inspiration, and a special thank you to Jennifer Fox-Proverbs for continuing the project with such dynamic and creative input. Thank you to Lin Clements, my editor, for her endless patience and wonderful attention to detail when editing the text and preparing the charts. A big thank you to Mia Farrant for her beautiful book design and gorgeous styling. Thanks also go to Cara Ackerman at DMC for providing me with threads and products from their exciting range. Thanks to Simon Whitmore for the wonderful photography which really makes the book look beautiful. Finally, as always, thank you to my lovely husband David and my wonderful family.

About the Author

Helen Philipps studied printed textiles and embroidery at Manchester Metropolitan University and then taught drawing and design before becoming a freelance designer. After working in the greetings card industry, Helen's love of needlecraft led her to create original designs for stitching magazines and later for books. Her work features regularly in *Crafts Beautiful, Let's Make Cards, Let's Get Crafting, Cross Stitcher* and *Cross Stitch Collection*. This is Helen's sixth book for David & Charles following on from *Cross Stitch Keepsakes* in 2008.

111

Index